DATE DUE			

Asleep in the Fire

Alabama Poetry Series

General Editors: Robin Behn and Thomas Rabbitt

Asleep in the Fire

Chard deNiord

The University of Alabama Press
Tuscaloosa and London

Copyright ©1990 by
The University of Alabama Press
Tuscaloosa, Alabama 35487-0380
All rights reserved
Manufactured in the United States of America

The paper on which this book is printed meets the minimum requirements
of American National Standard for Information Science-Permanence of
Paper for Printed Library Materials, ANSI A39.48-1984.

Library of Congress Cataloging-in-Publication Data

DeNiord, Chard. 1952–
    Asleep in the fire / Chard deNiord.
        p.   cm. -- (Alabama poetry series)
    ISBN 0-8173-0489-4 (alk. paper). -- ISBN 0-8173-0490-8 (pbk. :
alk. paper)
    I. Title. II. Series.
    PS3554.E532A9 1990   89-20459
    811.54--dc20   CIP

British Library Cataloguing-in-Publication Data available

For Liz

Acknowledgments

Nimrod
   The Woman Clothed with the Sun
The Iowa Review
   From the Apocrypha of David
   Hester
   The Wind and the Door
The American Poetry Review
   Zephyr
The Antioch Review
   Graffito
Tar River Poetry
   Horse Heart
Mid-American Review
   Fire Road
The Chester H. Jones Foundation, *The National Poetry Competition Winners 1987* (Honorable Mention)
   The Suet Feeder
The *Black Warrior Review* and *Anthology of Magazine Verse & Yearbook of American Poetry 1985*
   Watching on the Railroad
The Bennington Review
   Solstice
CutBank
   No Moon
   The Death of a Cow
Stone Country
   Recovery
Negative Capability
   Swimming Lesson
Piedmont Literary Review
   Crow
The Bad Henry Review
   Beyond Greenwich

Earthwise
MU 10 under the title The Enemy of Poetry
Insomnia
The Litchfield County Times
River Crossing
Fire Road

Contents

I. Winter Knowledge

II. Distant Steel

III. The Woman Clothed with the Sun

Asleep in the Fire

I slept but my heart was awake.
Song of Songs 5:2

I
Winter Knowledge

The Wind and the Door

On stormy nights he thinks
of the wind and door as lovers
destroying each other.
He has meant to plane an edge
for months so it will close,
but he feels he would miss the sound
of it banging against its hinge,
then remaining open in silence like a sail,
propelling the house beyond the town
to wild events in open fields.
It's as if it falls when it closes,
returning in a lull to its jamb.

He is happy this way in the interim,
falling asleep each night
in exactly the same way.
If the door breaks, he'll buy another,
or better yet, fix it.
He will take perfect measurements of its width
and length and examine its damage of splinters
with gentle hands.
He will mold it back into shape,
then wait for the heat of summer
to expand it again.
Until the door blows off
on a sleepless night,
he will take advantage of conditions.

Zephyr

That's "somewhere" outside the window passing
behind the couple on the train at dinner:
hills and fields, an occasional farm
with crops that reach beyond the sill.
He lights a cigarette and takes a closer look;
she is wounded beneath her dress, holding her side,
discussing the weather in San Francisco.
The wound in her side is where God last touched her.
"Oh, she is my sunshine!" says the man to himself
and the passing conductor. "My perfect pomegranate!"
He is aware before he is aware, streaming toward Denver,
another happy man from the Lord's imagination.
"This man is too happy," sayeth the Lord.
"I will appear closer to the window."
They give their orders: steak and sole.
This waiting together on the move, in two places
at once, like a jet beyond its boom, reveals
the sky on earth, as children say on Sunday mornings
after church: "The sky is at your fingertips,
not only up there, which means that it's also blue
down here." The train is like a doctor
leaning back, or a new mother with baby
at breast in her rocking chair, or a television
on wheels, or a showroom of televisions tuned
to the Nevada desert. Suddenly, the historian
is only important in this Gestalt for the way
he holds his pen and speaks to his wife.
Finally, too quickly, dinner arrives on china plates.
The rhyme of cutlery speaks for their teeth.
Wind and steel gird their loins.
They are like gazelles in another life,
wise at last after ages of talking with subtle beasts,
devoutly quiet, a perfect match.
The train disappears from under their seats,
and they are joined as one above the cactus,
and then the Rockies, and then the plains.

4

Graffito

Someone wrote *fuck* in the snow across
the soccer field at the primary school—
feet that leapt from huge sign to huge
sign, and then escaped: no trace of virgin
steps departing from the stiff support
of capital K.
            He must have covered them
or simply ascended above the backstop,
which is where he ended.
                    It was a boy because
it's always a boy who loves his mother but cannot
have her and feels compelled to find another.
The power of a girl lies within her showing
boys what else to write, and where salvation
is.
   But back to the field's deflowered snow . . .
The curious thing is that neither teacher nor parent
has scrambled the word with heavy boots, or altered
the F to P.
            It has remained into March,
only a trace visible now from the road
when ground breaks through the cover like open wounds.

Winter Knowledge

We were unclear about a time to meet;
without you here at dusk, I am left to gaze
at beauty's need: icicles on the bluff
and early darkness.
                     Runnels surge beneath
the bridge.
               They are the slow immaculate streams
of vengeance.
              A fire ignites above the ice
and burns your absence.
                  It is a sign that the heart
consumes the winter like a bride.
                      It is
a solitary flame.
            Nothing is lost.
I fear the river would have run without
a word, lured us in over time,
if we had been together.
                We must continue
to miss each other from time to time, build in
the inconvenience of misunderstanding,
then linger for a while on the nearest rail.
I cannot continue my search for you across
the fields without this strange desire.
                   I cannot
raise my voice to call out your name in the hills
if I already know where you are.

No Moon

The stars are slightly off, a child's rendering.
I don't want to make something out of nothing
but I can't help it; they are beasts and people and souls
and they can do whatever they want up there.
They are what makes night the opposite of modesty.
They are like the bison of Lascaux, fixed in motion,
grazing across my field of vision without a sound.
If cavemen drew from memory, holding their coals
with feminine ease while hunger accomplished
the rest, rehearsing their hunts on the stone cold walls
of deepest recess, then so can I, I tell myself,
but why and on what?
The stars are screaming with clues, forbidden to tell.
I am a child beneath them, beginning over, as if forever.
I am connecting them where I will.

Five hundred millenia later, I am glad as I lie here
that I cannot put all the fires out.
My father left them burning in the corners of my eyes
as if for a reason, as if for the stars,
and my mother constantly fueled them.
They are eternal discriminating fires.
They are not what makes me American but alive,
and you are the same. I take a last look up
before closing my eyes; now the stars are sheep
who have fallen in a well, cast down, though up, by
    counting.
The children are asleep nearby, breathing in time.
Outside the camp, two gems of animal eyes peer in
at the dying coals, mesmerized and bright.
They are hungry for the food and buried garbage,
daring enough to trample over us in the middle of the night.
I fear their coming and fall asleep.

From the Apocrypha of David

I wish I could die like Moses
gazing at the Promised Land.
I envy him that death atop Mt. Pisgah,
so scenic and self-fulfilling.
Lying here now beneath my palms
I ache inside from more than gout.
My palace is a huge luxurious joke.

As if my dotage weren't enough reward,
I am haunted by giants and women—
the women appear
whenever I dream
and laugh at everything I have to say.
I remember them in every detail,
their blemishes, their smiles.
They are Lilith, I know, ageless,
still beautiful, destroying my mind.
They are naked bathers
who love the sun.
They are married women
with husbands at the front.
They are a wilderness
without a mountain or any way out.

As for the giants,
there's usually just one,
but sometimes another, his identical twin.
They pretend to be dead
face down in the dust
but then stand up
with their severed heads raised high like trophies.
I wonder what else I have to do to kill them
for good.
My servants tell me they're just a dream.

Sheol is like a weight around my neck.
Why couldn't I at least have died
with Jonathan—he was so young
and dearer to me than any woman.
Have I lived so long
only to see my family disintegrate?
Absalom slain and Tamar raped?
If I had known my life would end like this
I would have stayed in the fields
and let my brothers go.

Samuel had a cursing eye
which Saul and Eli knew
but how was I to know,
still just a boy with only a lyre
and stupid courage?

"Sing to us, old king," the women cry,
"we long to hear your broken heart
before it stops."
Anything to chase them out.
My wind is short
but my mind still sharp.
"Love just one," I repeat.
"One either burns or he doesn't.
I have loved you all as one.
Forgive me, but you seemed that way,
unlike God.
Your faces were different but opened
the same.
I have suffered from this all my life,
gazing at Sharon through pretty eyes.
It didn't seem to matter at the time,
one God, one woman, one life.
I failed one of these
and therefore all."

My servants have sent for a beauty today
to test my strength.

Her name is Abishag.
I brought it on myself.
I will let them bring her to me
if they must.
It makes a good story.
Finally I'm not ashamed.
What better way to abdicate my crown?

I remember my childhood friends
and the back streets of Bethlehem
and the pasture's steps of grazing trails
and the songs I sang to sleepless Saul
and the jokes that Jonathan and I used to tell
and the one thing I'll never tell:
how slaying Goliath awakened my lust,
my monstrous love born of a lucky shot
and better kept a secret for the record's sake.
But what I felt there, looking down
on his unconscious body was my first holy desire,
my groin uncoiling to my core.
Mercy left me then, and I cut off his head.
Though impotent now, I can still recall
how the sight of him detached from his shoulders,
bloody and pagan, entered my soul like a woman.
From then on the two would be the same,
although I could never say this, especially to a woman.
I am thinking, however, of telling Abishag
since the last should know.

The Shepherd

I lie here forgiven beneath
the mansion white we decided on,
not moving until you move closer.
I can see my eyes in the slow roll
of their grief; darkness has fallen
behind the curtains.
I can hear the bleating of my unfound sheep.
I kiss you on the neck and lips.
I imagine my lambs in the dangerous hills
outside of town.
I hold your body next to mine and dream
then wake, dream then wake.
They are in the clutches of wolves by now,
dying so I may sleep with you.
They are the necessary kill of godly beasts,
staining the grass with crimson blood.
I am loving you again with each half of my heart.

The Past Is a Mistress

The past is a mistress with a lost address.
The night takes back her pretty face, reruns
her walk on a damaged screen then stops.
                                    I remember
her playful touch across my hand instead
of her kiss, a detail from a dream that lay undressed
for years beneath a sheet inside my head,
and of course the already tragic look in her eyes
that said, "Something's falling inside of me
to earth."
            This is the past as it turns out,
not the repeated scenes of love that the mind
projects in cenotaphs of light.
                                    She must
return on her own in a dream, unbidden and free
of need, as real as Nausicaa on the beach.
How easy then to mistake a dream for heavenly
light, a blessed face for *a blessed face.*

Hester

She knows where you can find her
outside of town, where nature argues
with God and a rabbit dies.
No homily can compare with her.
You are convinced by beauty first,
forgetful to death of its reward.
You are convinced in your heart by her walk
through the trees and her choice of songs.
You are cruel immediately and chase her down.
She is reluctant to talk to you,
but she turns around like an angel trapped
inside a dream.
You want to make love to her again
on the forest floor in order to remember
the first time, in order to damn
yourself in the woods beneath the passive eyes
of maple leaves, but your lips are burned
and you cannot kiss her.
You are torn and stare at the trees
which carry a wind of indifference:
"It's up to you."
She agrees.
You leave her there and return to your room.
The doom you write depends on confession.

Recovery

This year the doctors have taught me to say,
"The world suggests a connection between events."
Last year I avoided using the word suggest.
It had no meaning for me then
since I thought unclearly in my own absolutes,
as if my mind as a last resort
were trying to calculate to the very last place
its own square root: me only, as one is to one,
but me times me,
until I suffered from grandiosity.

I thought my marriage to a woman
I wasn't sure I loved
was more than coincidental
to the plague of caterpillars
that spring.
Because there was no reason
to believe, there was.

Two springs have passed since then
both full and green
and I have learned to think objectively again.
Suggest and coincidence straddle my tongue.
My wife is grateful and tapes the trees each April
to catch the worms at their ascent.
I would say I know more about my love
but now these are the words I dare not say.

Four Postcards from America

For Naomi Wallace

1

There is a harsh utility to this weather
since you left; all day it roves
in gray migrations across my window
until it reflects inside like a mirror
and I see you as you were behind a glass
with moving lips divorced from words.
So this is the present, obsessed with loss.
When I imagine your hair you disappear.
Your voice follows as if you were here,
trailing your departure at the speed of sound.
I memorized your reason in a foreign language.

2

To call it abandonment would be wrong.
You can tell what I am thinking.
Loneliness attacks our spirit with the look
of failure; this future would forget the time
we beat good-bye with a love whose hands
were paralyzed. In this way I let you go,
gripping with my too real hands LaGuardia's rail.
Acceptance doesn't mean you don't have to feel.
I am just learning this love which is why
I appear unready at times.
"Love is pointless," you said, "that stays confused."
So we called it friendship.

3

But if you would know, my deeper love
had only a deal at heart: my quick understanding
for your return. Now that you're gone,
I have grown religious with waiting.
Dreams are an idea for waking, but none has worked
so far: once in Reading waiting for the train,
once in Crete walking on graves.
Wherever we are it's like old times

before he arrived with renovated wrecks.
If I could grow angry at him I would,
but he is like history with looks, innocent
if deadly, the new object of your love.
I better stop before I think we failed.
Already I can hold my breath while breathing.

4
This love is violent that goes unused.

Letter from Stony Creek

With time at bay the water glistened beyond
the reeds, in memory first then sight: the sound.
The drive fanned above, colliding scope.
Beyond the quarries, hummocks trembled at passing
trains, or when you jumped tympanums beat.
Further on, a damnable distance didn't
retreat, spurring us on to cross over
the weir to fields of sea grass.
                                    Looking out
to sea, I found I was barred from getting here
from there, from leaving my body for any reason.
Low tide, we crossed the muck barefoot
to mammoth boulders—foreheads deep in thought.
You taught me names: glasswort, scrub and rose hip.
I tried to remember the following day, but couldn't;
my mind was on the man above the waves—
"the pier," you said.
                                    I gazed into the depths
of harbor rock beyond the peel of lichen.
I could have drowned in there with swimming eyes,
stared for days into the maw of granite.
I read a difference into the light of Sunday
evening, although it shined the same off distant
slate, flashed like flames across the water.

The Thin Path

The quiet I keep on the thin path
to the beach is the hardest.
                    The sound
of your talk below and the waves unrolling
against the shore of broken stones
is an oracle, my future now
of loving you.
            I am caught beneath
the tilt of maples and cry of difference
between ten thousand things: leaf
and stone, rail and wave,
me you.
        I feel old
in this descent, naming blossoms
along the trail: hyacinth, lilac,
and roses.
        I feel a table has
been righted in my heart, and I
am ready now to place a vase
at its center with a single flower.

II
Distant Steel

The Death of a Cow

I had just finished seeing my life again
in the blind of the dangerous curve
when I came upon them.
I was rounding the dangerous curve
on Holcomb Rock when a posse of farmers
in pickups put up their hands to stop me.

It was brown, big, and alive,
half-submerged in front of the culvert
through which the normally gentle Judith Creek ran.
I rolled down the window and peered out through
the interference of rain; their bodies
were forms, almost alien, in the familiar terrain
as they struggled to pass the thick ropes down
to Ed and Jim who then tied them securely
in bowlines around its midsection, a cow.

The waters, rising fast, cut through
their skin and whirled in panic.
The odds against them were rising fast
as they put their slippery blistered hands
to the task, as though they were saving themselves.
The cow seemed to bring them out to themselves
with her dumb high head lowing away
and the whites of her eyes which mirrored
her milk and thereby the one clear thread
of livelihood that ran like a blessing
through their lives.

Watching on the Railroad

When the water pipe below the farm
was still intact, routing a bluff-side spring
onto the riprap of the C&O,
I never dared jump on the long black trains
heaped with coal,
despite their pausing for the signal at Holcomb Rock.
The long hard run of track pointing in each direction
away from home, Ohio to the west
and Chesapeake to the east,
faded to vanishing point.
Men walked the tracks then,
mostly blacks from Coleman Falls,
now gardeners in town
with golden Hamilton watches
and Buddha-like faces at the bus stops.

Their shirtless backs shone in the sun
as they put down their picks
and rinsed the dull tin cup
three or four times before drinking.
I hid behind the elephant-skinned beech
twenty paces down and listened to them rail
about the heat and their work and the ache
in their backs.
I watched them walk away on the sleepers
through the eye of the tracks'
distant steel.

Sleep Out

My punishment is greater than I can bear.
                    Cain

A light by the barn revealed a bag, I thought,
of a man who left it there by the door then went
inside to sleep on the lam.
                    Tires screeched
on the curve above the field.
                    I was afraid,
fingering the grass, imagining the man inside
the loft with one eye open like Polyphemus.
The stars were scattered like devil's teeth.
                    An owl
inquired somewhere in the woods and lilacs bloomed
with danger.
                    I closed my eyes to see his face:
the same as mine beneath his beard.
                    His clothes
were a tattersall of others.
                    He asked again
about his brother.
                    "Yes," I answered, "you are."
But he didn't hear; he had borne his mark too far.
He raised his arm to kill again.
                    I burned
down the barn inside my head.
                    There was smoke
in the sky when I opened my eyes.
                    I had been dreaming
while a front moved in.
                    It was morning and
the bag was gone.

Trying to Forget

I am rounding the corner of Grand and Elm.
An aroma grazes the walk.
It's canoles.
Almost home in the whiplash of 5.
I have been good.
I have been good.
I'm telling this to the maple trees
and telephone poles.

I am walking slowly through the city,
hanging a mirror in front of me
on two shiny sky hooks.
I am trying to forget
the accident I have just seen
by talking to myself, going backwards
over my mental asterisks: unwritten letters,
dinner, the grocery list.
I am remiss about not going more often
to our lovely museums.
I am looking in the mirror and practicing
my identity scale: do, say, me,
when a train passes by underneath
on its way up from Coscob.

The bridge shakes as silver streams beneath,
a comet's tail toward Union Station.
I want to be on board discussing Vatican II
with a pretty girl from Stonington.
I will have just read up on it at last
and have a lively understanding of altar rearrangements
and the doctrine of Humanae Vitae.
Caboose, caboose, caboose.
The tracks are left immaculately clean.

I turn to the east, as if from regret,
to look beyond the city.

I conjure a scenario of sloops in the sound:
the wind backs down as they come about.
Their gull-white sails are mystical sheets
inviting me to fall
asleep standing up, keeping watch for new worlds.
From out there, distance distills the land
into the illusion of a sea above the sea.

The general qualm of city fare
is at its peak: stream of steady homegoing
past the familiar unfamiliar,
elementary my walk past the Green
beneath the sway of dying elms,
gum on my shoe, boards on the windows
of slated homes.

Twenty years ago this summer
I failed at lanyards but mastered the noose
to no avail.
At twilight, I watched a cabal of older boys
kick a can as they went over their plans for a riot.
Too eager to join them against
the grain of my growing
I screamed riot before they did.
For that I hung
on the chin-up bar beneath the moon the moon.

I continue walking, a victim of proverbs,
across the grid of backbreaking cracks.
I picture my mother in her garden, as if for luck.
Here, on Grand Avenue the beauty of things
as they are is clear:
a blue Jaguar, the smell of canoles.

Hull Pond in January

For Rayna

A small figure out on the ice grows
smaller against the distance, not quite
skimming yet, slide-stepping into
harmless pratfalls—a blade gone
errantly out or in against the inductive
of balance.
        "Not too far!" her mother calls.
The ice is thick.
        Across the lake an auger
drills infinitely into the crust.
Trout swim slowly around in their sleep
like morals in a callous heart.
        The figure
feels them under his feet and decides to drill
there; no, there.
        The sky, darkening, slows
or so it seems in the January light, then halts
altogether.
        A sheet of cold
ascends the ice to form a zone between
her skates and voice.
        The surface freezes deeper,
then shifts against the banks, cracking down
this winter's spine from one end to the other.

Tree Time

For Soren

The time had come again like a voice down
the hall to close my book and listen to
his plea:
        "Let's get the tree today."
                        His timing,
his wonder awakening mine grown dim again
like morning ice. He pulled me up by the hands
and balanced me there transfixed, a father's trick.
I stared at the snow around the sill.
                        He fetched
my things from the laundry room, and when I still
didn't move, he helped me on with my coat.
I stood like a tree in a stand, imagining
a man on the edge of a cold platform, brooding.
Once "ready"—not me—he led me like a blindfolded friend
to the door.
           "Now where are you taking me?"
I asked. "Do you know?"
                    "There's a sign down
the road for trees. I'll show you."
                      We travelled
in silence to the turn.
               "A deer!" he cried.
"Over there! Leaping! Now!"
                  "Where?"
"He's gone."
           "Are you sure?"
                  "Yes. A big one with horns.
You never see."
           I turned the radio on:
Sinatra.
          "Change it, Dad."
                I left it on.
He should hear this voice amidst the snow
at Christmas time—a voice by which to change
his mind when grown as I remembered then

my father's tuning in to Danville's easy
listening, dreaming secrets I have come
to know from sitting and waiting and walking
through snow. I knew I couldn't tell him a thing
about trees, or why I couldn't see
beyond them: how eager I was to grow blind
to the things of this world, while continuing
to see. How similar he would become.
Because he didn't yet know or care
about another world I turned to him
at the hopeful bend and spoke his holy language:
"Let's find this farm *today* and cut a tree!
A tall one this year that sweeps the ceiling.
A beautiful spruce all around. A homeless pine!"

Lost Saw

. . .go freely with powerful uneducated persons . . .

Walt Whitman

Gone suddenly in the midst of work,
our saw, vanished, in a pocket of Piedmont heat.
Charlie swore that it was stolen because
it disappeared.
        "Nothing disappears,"
he claimed. A wrench returned last winter though
like a prodigal of air.
        "Returned," he said.

"No more posts until we find the thing."

Two customers in Madison Heights were waiting
for their promised loads of a hundred each.
I filed for theft and bought a new Macullough
with stainless teeth and automatic choke.
The locust fell like sleep throughout the summer.
We played the breeze and physics of trunks, then piled
a load onto the Ghost, a vintage Chevy,
and drove away in the smoke of Swisher Sweets.

I forgot the saw that disappeared,
while Charlie dreamed against his notion of theft.
He knew that blaming friends prevented them
from getting close. I was different for being
the owner's son. With his accusing done,
he set to dreaming and forgetting, dreaming and forgetting,
the vision he tried to have of finding it
by thinking of something else; how, for instance,
to hide a woman beneath his bed, or where
to dig for a spring. It will come to me,
as the others have, he said to himself at night.
He was only honest when talking to himself about
his tools and metaphysics. His friends were forced
to wait a month of sleeps, and sometimes forever.

Two months had passed since Bud was down, so I
was curious to find him there one Sunday morning
in early fall with rod in hand, smiling
his simple smile from ear to ear. When something
was found he'd come back down to fish with Charlie
beside the James and talk of fish and sales
and the humid weather, but never a word of trans-
migration; the fish could hear the slightest whisper.
Each time they'd catch enormous carp and make
their peace, then carry the meat across the river
to the hungry children of famous men.

                             "Remember
that saw," Charlie said. "It's come back to me."
Bud stood still in the door holding the carp.
"Last night, in a dream I saw it in the barn,
just where we left it and couldn't recall, beneath
that beam collapsed from the loft." He reached
behind the open door of his mobile home.
"Well here she is, no worse from wear." He glanced
at Bud and said, "It's strange, however, she didn't
rust a little in there. I waited for you
to start her up. What do you say she starts
right up?"

              "You know she'll start right up," Bud
proclaimed. Charlie pulled the cord with ease
at first, then quickly in sudden jerks until
she choked and caught. He held it up on open
throttle, then turned to some trees of paradise
with a smile that bared his bargain teeth and sunk
her chain into the pulp of the giant weed.

Memory Gardens

They're spraying hog urine on the fields today.
You can smell it twenty five miles away.
It casts a pungent smell that lingers for hours.
It gathers inside the barns, saffron and steaming,
streaming in gallons down built-in channels
to reservoirs beneath the floor.

Outside of town in the nursing home
a hundred faces appear at the windows
like Christmas flames.
They are growing dangerously close
to nothing with a passion;
Grant Wood, the painter, was right.
They are hypnotized by the tractor's ambling
back and forth across the rows,
and finally they are glad to smell this powerful smell
above their own,
although they would call it their own.

Operation

I stood as still as a sleeping bird upon
my stool. The problem lung was stained
with tar and barely rising—a torpid thing
like a bottom fish without its fins.
"This is what happens," my father said.
I dreamed of catching the frog-like heart
between my hands to keep my blood on course.
I dreamed of climbing into the hole
and telling my "sins" of slaughtering
squirrels inside their nests,
of killing a flicker at her trove of vermin,
of lifting the skirts on screaming girls.
This patient's soul would be my priest
behind the curtain of flesh and sleep,
and I would be forgiven upon his waking.
A cloud of stars and deep unknowing
filled my head beneath the lamp, unpinned
my knees. I clutched a gown to keep
from falling into the quick of his incision.
"You've contaminated me!" he said
from behind his mask; his eyes conveyed
the danger. I hadn't imagined the sterile needs
of an open chest. I couldn't imagine being
forbidden to touch my father who hadn't risen
or even died, who was a stranger now
on the other side of this inhuman table.
The nurses watched like Muslim wives.

Solstice

This evening has sent its swiftest hoplite
to me with the message that he has tired
from speeding against the speed of grass
and is now going to lie down exhausted
and die without a word of victory. I need
a word of victory to face this longest night.
I must remember without thinking
as a kind of natural check, my human trick
for enduring winter, no less than the bear's.

I play back the time I descended a Rocky Mountain.
I recall the dream-like verve with which I slalomed
toward the clock-wise river;
first, lickety split on parka silk,
ass-first down the snowy sluice
from Red Cloud's summit, we slid
to tree-line.

Farther down, the narrow logs across the gully
aroused a sultry balance: take to heart
then foot this backhanded majesty, take to heart
then ear the happy thrashing sound of bivouac
playing its crash of notes to aspen snare.
Take to groin the dangerous height cracking
your safe left and right with the touch of dare.

Although I always awake before I hit,
I allow myself in this evening dream to land
at river's edge without a mortal injury.

Horse Heart

1

She dropped to her side and began
to heave in fits of poison,
whether weed or snake, I couldn't tell.
It was my first witnessing of death
so I didn't know how it came or when.
"She will die tonight," my father,
the surgeon, said, then went inside.
I stayed until dusk, imagining her eyes
fall with the dark, and her nostrils flare
with final breath.
Perhaps a hoof would kick the dirt
and she would die like that.
Night enshrouded her inside the field
like a doctor pulling up the sheet.
Hosts of gnats swirled above her matted hide
and sucked her lids for easy blood.
How I hated the owl's country song just then,
so repetitive and hollow.

2

I saw her close her eyes in my sleep
and exhale her galloping self,
exchanging this air for another.
I kicked her legs which stood
in vain with rigor mortis, then opened her lids
to find her eyes turned to isinglass.
I wondered about the the rest of her now—
what death had done—so I cut her open
at the abdomen and took her apart, organ
by organ until I came to her heart.
I was tempted to make it an oracle or charm.
I was tempted to ask for a wish in return
for seeing to a proper burial.

Anything then to become a man.
I carved it out and washed it clean
with the hose, until its blood was gone.

Madison's Ridge

I twisted off a hemlock stem which clung
and clung in stubborn strips.
"Stop in the name of love!" I sang
as I wound its skin to shreds,
then pulled it clean, baring its bone.
The knack down, I did the same with other stems,
flinging them out beyond the fashion of branches.
Their hemorrhage bled a clear inflammable blood
which stuck to my hands, staining my lines.
"More! More!"—the word kept coming.
Only the sight of branches floating earthward
like snow, the snow of these very mountains
in winter, kept me going.
I had dreamt all day of sleeping well
on Madison's ridge, in the mountainous dark.

III
The Woman Clothed with the Sun

Devotion

I have been considering the lilies of the field,
how they neither toil nor spin.

I have been picking street glass
out of my feet.

I am glad for walking but envious of roots.
I get the Lord's logic but not his meaning,

which is why he teaches me to consider
the natural beauty of dumb objects,

how my soul is connected to them.
My heels are bleeding as much from my considering

as from the glass.
I want to know what Julian was doing

in the interim between her "showings,"
how she toiled and spun with contemplation,

following the rules of knowing
that God's essential being partakes in us

but not we in him.
I am consoled by my geranium

which sits in glory beside my bed.
Its leaves are the ears

of the dead listening to my complaints
with perfect patience, defining

existence by default:
You are only yourself in another world.

When I imagine its growth as laughter
I am offended, and hate the dead,

although I do anyway.
When I imagine its growth as grief

I grow too, and love the dead,
although I do anyway.

When I don't imagine its growth at all
I measure its stalks in millimeters

and wash its leaves, and fertilize its soil,
and stare into its stamen and pistil

with curious eyes, and take the dead for granted,
although I do anyway.

It sits beside my bed in a ray of sun
emitting a pungent smell around the sill.

It neither speaks nor sings,
but blooms with flowers

which I take to be tragic answers.

Swimming Lesson

Yesterday, the waves reminded me of sinners
falling to their knees at Mass.
I looked again and didn't see anything
this time that wasn't there.
This was vanity, I knew, my only crazy
consolation for seeing things as they are.
I swam this morning like an angel, executing
strokes of beatitude through clouds of foam.

I stuck my head beneath a wave this afternoon,
stared up, then down.
Once my father stepped away from the stairs
and let me fall.
He had caught me twice with loving arms.
"Let that be a lesson," he said.

I was floating like that again,
only not through the air.
The lodes were cracks and the fish the stars
that swam around when I opened my eyes.
I held my breath for as long as I could,
until my memory of the blood was clear,
the small round puddle in front of the open door.

I wished to hold my breath forever,
remembering my birth, swimming away
at my human pace. I wished to see
the flukes of whales muscling by
within reaching distance,
but I had used my air like a ticket.
The surface was lost from underneath
as I rose to breathe the sky.

Crow

A crow can see through a man like Jesus,
in an instant, before he reaches for his gun.
She rises mythically, breaking the silence
of evening with her pure black voice
as if silence itself were being scratched
by utter necessity, as if our sins
were being taken in for careful inventory.

No matter which way I look at crows
I always see them the same,
as large black birds sitting in trees
with a frightful knowledge of movement,
as former carp immune to lures,
as fanatical followers of a modern creed
which says, "That which moves is probably alive
and therefore dangerous."

Beyond Greenwich

Beyond Greenwich now I stare
at southern Connecticut yawing outside my window
like a diorama slide show: northeastern industry,
tenements, and belfry spires pricking the sky
like straightaway tracks on a long incline.
One wonders from this industry when
and how the Puritans lost their dream,
and what became of the Grand Errand,
and whose sweet songs dulcified the Great Awakening.
By the mere looks of things, I would say offhand
that it was their know-how, their sinful know-how,
their genius. What else?
Witness now this latest plan
of laying the eastern corridor
with concrete sleepers and sectional track
for a smoother, faster ride.
The patented beat of a heavy heart is gone,
increasing my fear of the in-between.

I cannot see ahead, only imagine
the shiny tracks winding toward New Haven
through Stamford, Darien, Fairfield, Bridgeport,
and Milford.
We are still moving
so my imagination must be right.
It is easy to think that I am still
and the world is moving.
It is easy to feel immune to time
when the train is early.

But the world is moving, despite
my wish for it not to, despite
this reality of spinning against my stillness
which will end at Union Station,
where I will have to walk
upon the pavement, eating my words.

And not only moving but revolving,
sloughing off generation after generation.
I am thankful for places to go
and condemn the doctrine of predestination,
for this progress is good and I know it.

Whatever the future is besides this blur
of ricketing mass, this face of glass
swimming with names, I am here
with my ticket ready, heading home.

The Suet Feeder

I've been watching the hanging suet
outside my window. For weeks it has hung
a disembodied brain inside its mesh,
attracting only occasional starlings
who leave their tooth marks daintily,
then fall away. For weeks it has hung without
diminishing, its lilac branch arching still
beneath the yellow deadness of its weight.
I keep hoping a cardinal will fix on it
and hack away for hours, picking its pulp.
I keep hoping a bird of paradise
will notice it from afar and leave
her precious mango feeders to fly
across the ages and Mesopotamia and modern oceans
and industrial parks and the South Bronx
and Love Canal and Time's Beach
and Three Mile Island and Silicon Valley
and the scars of freeways linking us all
to land upon my grotesque offering
with a hunger unheard of in paradise.
The sight of it clinging with talons
would thrill me as I watched it gorge itself
and fall to the ground.
I would sympathize with it there
before the cats arrived, born to fly
but too fat to rise.
I would compare the slippage in my eyes
and muscles to its inertia, recalling
in vain my former quickness above the rim.
I would give up my telephone and car
to see one pretty bird at the suet.
I would fall asleep at my altar
to lure one godly bird from her nest in the sky.

River Crossing

When I stopped in the middle of the river barefoot
and hot from running to the top of Steep Rock Park
the world stopped too, or so it seemed.
         The straight
gold hands of the village clock beyond
the ridge continued to move in their usual ruse
of passing hours.
      There were weightless motes
in the sun-filled air, rising like the souls
of fired bodies.
     I stood on a carpet of moss
that lay beneath the shallow water and forgot
my run, already home.
      Here I was in the current
of heaven listening to the catbird sing.
The trees along the banks exceeded numbers,
danced like girls to the psalm of memory.
Three clouds waved in in the shape of hands.
The clock beat out its time.
      I stepped again
from rock to rock to reach the port of other
side, safe from revelation.
     Only
then did the sun send down its slashing orders.

Song of Saul

Now for my war on evening hunger
and radio's lure at twelve.
I listen through the screen
like a bear who wakes in spring
with terrible hunger: the sound
of a breeze and then the rain.
They are my brain at work outside
itself in the open air.
I am soothed by the voice
of that gifted child beside
my bed who blesses the bats
at the heart of night.
I would not tell him the horrors
of faith this close to sleep—
what holy rage despised the
cry of salvaged sheep.
It is not darkness that frightens
me but waning light.
I open my arms to the witch
of Endor. I feel the names
of the dead on polished stone.
This is not insomnia but regret.
This is not a malady
as some who flourish against
the decorous wall might suggest,
but knowledge of the bones
behind our bones: the dust.
A song reduces the guilt of tiredness.
A song bends back the arm of memory.

The Thirty Years' War

It begins in the dark
with a window breaking in stillness.
Night blows through the loss
and swallows home.
The other windows break inside themselves
but keep their face of glass.
Their echo carries across the fields,
sounding off the neighbors' barns.
It is a litany of prayers and shifting ice.
It is the shatter of defenestration.
Inside the house, dawn arrives
at a critical angle.
A nimbus shines around the mullions:
"This is war."
It takes the glass ten thousand years to heal.

Priest

He stands on the edge
    of the world
with a thousand other shoppers
    staring down at the darkness
where the only sound
    he hears is the fall
of steel extensions sliding
    through themselves but never
reaching a ground.

He imagines this darkness
    as the backside of light
through which the fields
    of pure abstraction lie.
It is a kind of earth
    in heaven where the grass
beneath the boring tree
    is cast in famous light.

The curb is a mountain
    on his daily walks
and he is falling.
    What faith is left inside
his heart since the prophecy
    of Lamentations?
What is he to think,
    like every man,
of God's contempt for death?
    What good is goodness
if evil is the test?

He is falling while standing up
    and sitting down.
He is falling while clipping
    a slew of coupons.
He is approaching the space

where earth and heaven meet:
the walk outside his gate,
    the bed he hardly makes.

He is praying for the sight
    of a perfect man in a golden dress
at the bottom of the ladder.
    Will the sections course to light?
Will his body survive
    the violent turn of stepping
off the curb and onto the street?

These are his questions
    since losing his vision
of tents and bleeding feet.
    He lost his fear
in the comfort of windows.
    He lost his passion
for sharpening swords and cursing trees.

He stops by a barrel
    encompassed by hands and throws
in a page to watch it burn.
    The flames restore his faith in man,
free up his soul to lift his legs
    onto the walk.

Inside a cave the enemy flashes
    a card with a splotch of ink
and says, "Now tell me what you think this is."
    "It is," he says, "the hole
inside my head.
    It is a woman without her body."

MU 10

You're in a forest.
Your doctor is lying on the ground
licking ants while you do jumping jacks.
He is listening to you
talk about your hatred of women.
You drag him for a while
in a straight direction,
until he realizes you are traveling in circles.
He comments on the nature of your circles:
"Some are oblong while others are round
and still others incomplete."
There is no way out,
so you hire a lumberjack to cut down
the forest, which is no problem.

He asks you why you have shaved your head.
"Perhaps you are in grief?"
He is frank when necessary, but sometimes late.
Now the sun is too bright, burning your skin.
You are also bleeding from your ribs.
A ranger finds you near death.
When you awake, you are still in the forest.
Your doctor sits beneath a parasol
in a seersucker suit.
He offers you some pills.
The sun goes behind a cloud.
You are tired but sane.
You put on a catalpa leaf
and pray for rain, which promptly comes.
He says you were aware of what you did
as only the tips of his cordovans get wet.
He allows you to feel guilty in an act of mercy
as the sun goes down behind his head.

Insomnia

If you lie awake at night
you must consider it your responsibility
to observe the stillness around you
as if it were a grand experiment
upon which the survival of mankind depended.
You must not deny your anger
at not being able to fall asleep,
then listen to the silence
as if it were a voice about to speak
in tongues about the coming light.
As for your anxiety,
you must allow it free reign inside your soul,
conceding your choice in the matter:
fear of entering the darkness's water,
fear of waking before you're out.
Without pen or paper,
you must watch the time pass infinitely slow
beside your bed,
as if it were stuck in a temporal jam,
the seconds creeping by,
and when the sun finally rises,
redefining your tiredness,
you must awake like everyone else
and face the day.

The Woman Clothed with the Sun

For Jorie Graham

She is driving beyond the country,
disdaining homes, heading home.
We are her hostages bound and gagged
on the passenger side.
She speaks to us like a friend:

I am speeding in celebration
of a recovery, happy again
to be pressing down on the pedal
with a healthy leg.
I can consider myself normal again
with things to do and places to go,
but such recovery is a lapse, you hear,
such recovery is fatal disease.
Look, these houses are trapped
between neatness and pride.

How lucky we are to be moving along.
Are you listening?
I am preparing us, three strangers,
for the time when we will wish
we had appreciated the bars of sun
on doctored lawns and the changing minds
of mothers at home.
There is a power inside this wheel
which plays too easily into my hands,
and yet I am not foolish about the olden days.
Red lights behind!
Let's lose them.

I am angry at flashing signs
and white noise and digital time,
set off like tinder on a burning crust.
Never again will I believe
that the smallest thing is the smallest thing,
even if it is: the rapine of circles today,

the impunity of numbers tomorrow.
There is a trap beneath your skin
through which a shadow will enter in the end
at the speed of light and find you brief.
It is as black as the garment hole
in Giotto's fresco of the crucified Christ.
The soul must enter there to have a chance
while the body smolders back to dust
and the wind records your name.
It is the empty chrysalis in which your flesh
will return at the appointed hour
like never before, immune to flames.

Can you hear the hush before the roar?
It is the sound of darkness rising.
It is the prelude to fire,
the necessary horror,
and only half of us is ready.
I say this as one who has tried again
and again to lose her faith.
Are we listening?
Perhaps today at midnight we will pray
for nothing else than to be together.

Route 7

There is no easy way to cross the river
south of Kent for a reason, but who will explain?
The towns and villages are losing their memory.
It is the end of another paschal century.
What New Light will move these drivers past
the bridge at cruising speed?
                                    Who still hears
the valley's echo off the cracked macadam?
"The same religious mind that trains the spirit
loves the spider."
                        What is the price for daily
jams beyond the connector?
                                    This strip is the way
of promised land, and we are not moving.
Judgment forms like a dream at the hand of questions,
and quickly I am changed, hanging from
a vine at the gate of heaven.
                                    The officer snickers
and gives me a ticket.
                        "We have undone
the curse of Babel," I tell him, "and finished the tower.
No faith exists in proving God correct."
He is not impressed and rides away on his Harley
Davidson.
            This, too, is a vision.
                                    Green
is moot at the busiest hour.
                                    My mind depends
on open lanes for wandering.
                                    The river
flows like a lullaby beneath the bridge,
but who can drive and sleep?
                                    We are absurd
in standing cars with horns that cannot sing.

Prophecy Against Those

They will grow ass's ears and stand
like guards at the funerals of their own mothers.

They will forget history as if it were
a bad memory they can live without.

They will become victims of their own crime
for losing their fear of the dark.

They will confuse art with eloquent despair.

They will be devoid of "crazy" leaps and other lives.

They will become famous for their towers.

They will pass eye exams year after year.

They will cease from studying tragedy
and find humor in violence.

They will dress sharply and abuse women.

They will deny their loneliness on the street
and hone their wit.

They will get ahead.

They will have no literature.

They will grow blind to the safety
of the avant garde and high absurd.

They will turn into boards
with infinite splinters.

They will misprize and misprize.

They will see no connection between
themselves and a hazelnut.

They will destroy the earth with luxuries.

They will recoil with disdain
at "darken with kindness."

They will take pride in their faithlessness
and win at the table.

They will depend on panels
and laugh at Orpheus.

They will sew lids to their lids
and carry knives to school.

They will lose the mouth
to their terrible hunger.

They will dream unceasingly of cocks crowing.

"N"

I am frightened by this beautiful day.
It is full of numbers which have grown
so long I can no longer count them.
I pull down the shades and put on a record,
then take it off. A beam of sun cuts
the sill and splays on the floor.
It is a scroll unrolled with the radiant news:
"I am the Word without letters.
I am the scanner of numbers."

I am afraid of seeing a squirrel killed
in the road, as I did yesterday, run over
on the broken line with its number etched
in black across its back in small italic numerals.
I am afraid I will look up
at just the wrong moment and see a sparrow
fall from the sky, surrendering its wings
to the air for marking.
And I am afraid of hearing the crow's omniscient caw
announcing the deaths of innocent victims.

Tomorrow will be cloudy, I hope, gray
as thunder, giving me time to regain my nerve.
I will take a walk up Hickory Hill in the rain,
then wait for the sun to emerge between the branches
of merciful trees, in the parish of shade.
I am tired of this fear. I miss the light
which shines as well upon the living.

The Sun Is a Razor

The sun is a razor on the lawn.
I am cut off in shadow, resigned
to evening. I am insanely right:
Darkness is in the cloak business.
Silence is the granddaddy
at the bottom of the lake.

Come talk to me neighbor's child
with your Tonka truck.
I see you as me in the fescue
infected with plastic men.
Save me, please, from such easy oversight.
Tell me the time and I will remember
that stillness wins like the tortoise.
Tell me your name and I will forget.
You rise above your house when I look away.
You are the man you want to be descending
to the ground, cutting your strings.
This double vision will preserve you
in another world, and I will have proved
my theory on love.
Your name will come to me.

The grass is sweating in the shadows
beneath the eaves.
There is no way to dream of women at will.
This perfect weather erases me.
I clear the street with a blink.
A colorless snake remains, clinging
to the curb, speaking Chinese.
It is immune to my imagination.
It is reality.

Come talk to me Mr. Ant, red and wiry,
and I will tell you that night is a miracle
because it finally occurs outside the Law,
at a moment when no one can see.

The Cape of Stillness

I close my eyes and the world falls into view.
Continents swirl below like souvenirs.
Silence speaks to me through voices that carry forever
in open space the awful global secret
that everyone tells and also keeps.
"Silence," I yell at the silence,
but it continues to whisper a thousand lies
about another kingdom.
I am afraid it is I who speak.

My mind engulfs this body and stares
at the sun, regaining its sight at darkness.
I bring myself back to its beautiful blindness,
at this sunny day, when a titmouse sings.
My imagination is this dangerous,
lifting me off from the cape of stillness.
I am afraid it is I who speak.

Tracks

Are holy leaves the Echo then of blisse?
  Echo: Yes.

George Herbert

Ten thousand steps precede me on the tracks,
then disappear around the bend where a sign
warns of danger: Falling Rocks.
A voice inside the rail proclaims: "You are
alone in the company of another world."
It is the song of the dead in general.
I call it the river chorus and sing along
like a corpse come back to walk from Stony Point
to Rusens.
            I am a master or slave with too many
regrets to enter heaven.
                      The earth is strong
with consolation, and I believe that heaven
depends on things to exist: the rail behind
the rail, the idea of gravel.
                      A man is left
no choice beside the James but to swing his arms
when he walks.
                  His hands are free in the jealous air.
The beauty alone of auburn current and restless
steers across the river stokes my eyes' stubborn
fever.
        There is no sense in the sight, and what
good God cools my head with His distant ear?

Fire Road

I saw your body rise above the trees, then walk
with me beyond my reach. You did not walk from place
to place, but disappeared in strides of light. I heard
you say, "Do not touch," although we always touch.
Your voice was deep inside the river; the river
roared that I was deaf. The sun declared that I
was blind. Because you led me off a trail when I
was young and willing then to follow you down
to a stream, "a song," you said, I heard the dead trees
whisper, "Your love remains inside the air like flesh."

About the Author

A graduate of Yale Divinity School and the Iowa Writers Workshop, Chard deNiord worked as a psychotherapist for five years in New Haven, Connecticut. His poems have appeared in the *American Poetry Review*, the *Black Warrior Review*, the *Iowa Review*, and *Nimrod*, and he was a scholar at the Bread Loaf Writers' Conference. Presently, he holds the endowed chair in religious studies and philosophy at the Putney School in Vermont.